LESSONS

David Carr Glover
and Jay Stewart

Design and Illustrations: Jeannette Aquino
Editor: Carole Flatau

FOREWORD

Teacher and Parents:

LESSONS, Level Two, from the David Carr Glover METHOD for PIANO reviews the basic concepts presented in LESSONS, Level One. New concepts are introduced and reinforced sequentially through the use of original compositions, folk songs and the sounds of today. This book, combined with the recommended supplementary materials, continues to assist the student in developing the ability to read and perform musically through interval recognition, sight reading and ear training.

The student will continue to experience the basic elements of improvisation as the creative activities, EXPLORE, are presented.

Supplementary materials are carefully correlated and coded with the LESSONS book to provide reinforcement of all concepts.

The David Carr Glover METHOD for PIANO has been created to provide an enjoyable program of piano instruction which is pedagogically sound. David Carr Glover and his collaborators wish you a happy, successful musical journey!

Supplementary materials correlated with
LESSONS, Level Two, from the
David Carr Glover METHOD for PIANO

Contents

Only WHOLE STEPS are used in this piece. LISTEN to the sounds of the whole steps as you play.

What does Moderato
mean?_____

ICE PALACE

GLOVER - STEWART

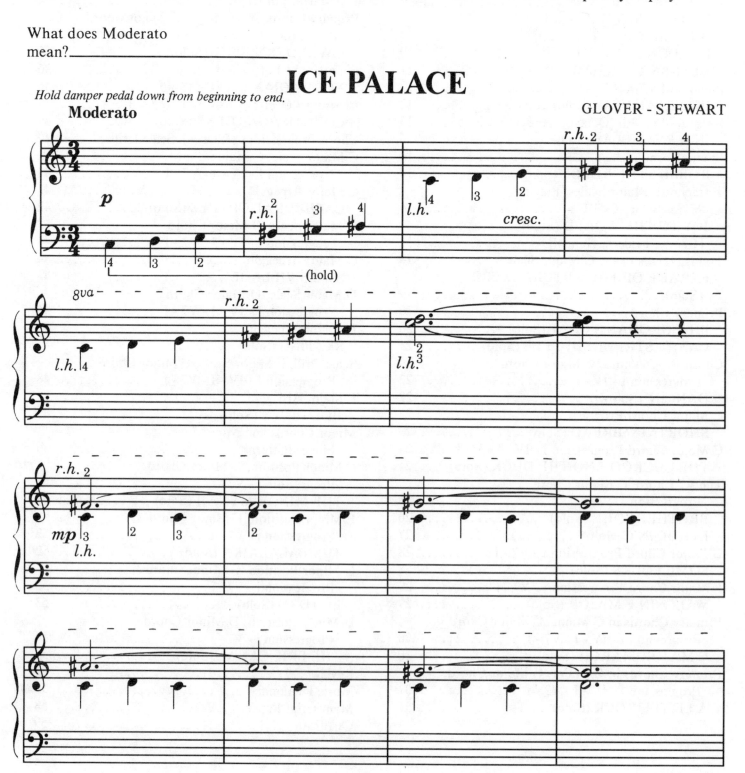

You are now ready for THEORY, Level Two, from the David Carr Glover METHOD for PIANO.

Interval of a 6th

When you skip 4 white keys, the interval is called a 6th.

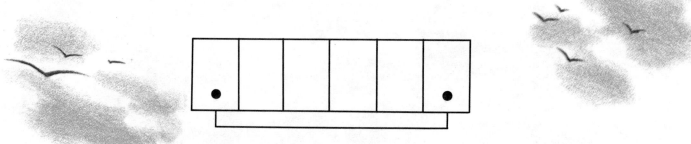

Play intervals of a 6th several different places on the keyboard. Use fingers 1 and 5 of each hand. LISTEN to the sounds of the intervals as you play.

Close your eyes and LISTEN as your teacher plays MELODIC and HARMONIC 2nds, 3rds, 4ths, 5ths, and 6ths. Use your EAR to identify the intervals. Each interval has a unique, distinct sound that you should learn to recognize.

An interval of a 6th on the staff is written from a line note to a space note, or from a space note to a line note.

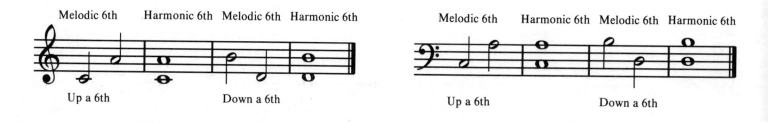

As you play these intervals, say their names.

INTERVAL PLAY

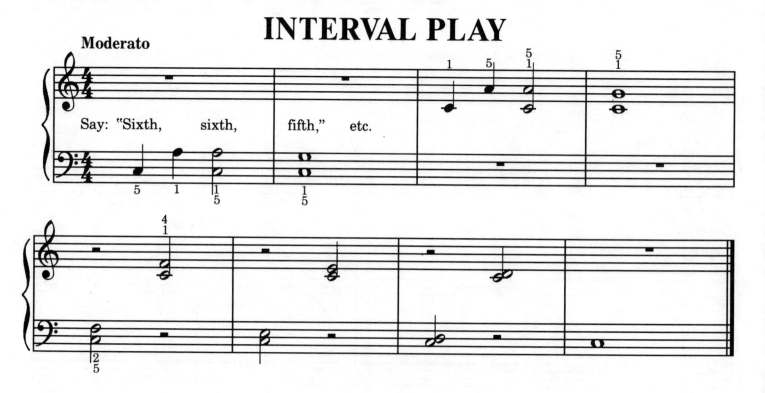

You are now ready for Level Two PERFORMANCE and Level Two SIGHT READING AND EAR TRAINING from the David Carr Glover METHOD for PIANO.

TONE BALANCE (Review)
Many times one hand will play louder than the other. This is called
TONE BALANCE.

Melodic lines are usually played louder than their interval accompaniments,
although this is not always indicated by expression marks. LISTEN for the
melodic lines to sing above the accompaniments throughout this book.

Play the interval of a 6th
by moving UP a WHOLE
STEP above the top key of
the Five Finger Position.

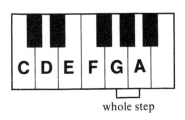

Practice this INTERVAL ACCOMPANIMENT before playing
"Prelude." Keep your eyes on the music. Do not look at your hands.

Memorize the above Interval Accompaniment, then play with your
eyes closed.

What does Adagio mean? _____

Key of _____ , Key signature _____

PRELUDE

GLOVER - STEWART

EXPLORE: Create a different sound. Change every E to E - flat and every A to A - flat.

The interval of a 6th may be played by moving DOWN a HALF STEP from the bottom key of the Five Finger Position.

Practice this INTERVAL ACCOMPANIMENT before playing "Skip to My Lou." Keep your eyes on the music. Do not look at your hands.

Memorize the above Interval Accompaniment, then play with your eyes closed.

Added lines and spaces above and below the staff are called LEGER LINES and SPACES. They extend (make larger) the staff.

Leger notes —— Middle C   B

What does Allegretto mean? _____

SKIP TO MY LOU

FOLK SONG

Swing your part-ner,   Skip to my Lou,   Swing your part-ner,   Skip to my Lou.

Swing your part-ner,   Skip to my Lou,   Skip to my Lou, my   dar - ling.

EXPLORE: Cross your right hand over your left hand and play the melody two octaves lower than written.

You are now ready for TECHNIC, Level Two, from the David Carr Glover METHOD for PIANO.

The Dotted Quarter Note

A dot placed after a note adds half the value of the note. A dotted half note receives 3 beats.

2 beats plus 1 beat (half the value of the note) = 3 beats

A DOTTED QUARTER NOTE (♩.) receives 1½ beats.

1 beat plus ½ beat (half the value of the note) = 1½ beats

A DOTTED QUARTER NOTE receives the same beat value as a quarter note tied to an eighth note.

1 beat plus ½ beat = 1½ beats

Clap and count aloud the following rhythm:

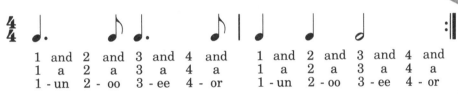

Your teacher will direct you in the preferred method of counting.

BRIDAL CHORUS

* RICHARD WAGNER (1813-1883)
arr. Glover - Stewart

* Richard Wagner, born in Germany, is considered to be one the world's greatest composers of opera.
"The Bridal Chorus" appears in his opera *Lohengrin.*

Practice this INTERVAL ACCOMPANIMENT before playing "London Bridge." Keep your eyes on the music. Do not look at your hands.

Memorize the above Interval Accompaniment, then play it with your eyes closed.

Key of _____ , Key signature _____

LONDON BRIDGE

FOLK SONG

Allegretto

Lon - don Bridge is | fall - ing down, | Fall - ing down, | fall - ing down.

Lon - don Bridge is | fall - ing down. | My fair | la - dy.

EXPLORE: Change the left hand interval accompaniment to quarter notes, alternating from the bottom note to the top note.

Example:  *etc.*

Practice this INTERVAL ACCOMPANIMENT before playing "Kum-ba-yah." Keep your eyes on the music. Do not look at your hands.

Memorize the above Interval Accompaniment, then play with your eyes closed.

Key of _____, Key signature _____

What does Andante mean? _____

KUM-BA-YAH

FOLK SONG

EXPLORE: Play the left hand accompaniment of this piece as you sing the melody (words or note names). DO NOT play the right hand. For excellent ear training, do this activity with several other pieces in this book.

Interval of a 7th

When you skip 5 white keys, the interval is called a 7th.

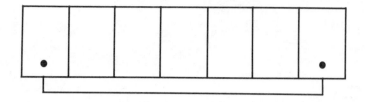

Play intervals of a 7th several different places on the keyboard. Use fingers 1 and 5 of each hand. LISTEN to the sounds of the intervals as you play.

Close your eyes and LISTEN as your teacher plays MELODIC and HARMONIC 2nds, 3rds, 4ths, 5ths, 6ths, and 7ths. Use your EAR to identify each of the intervals. Each of the intervals has a unique, distinctive sound that you should learn to recognize.

An interval of a 7th on the staff is written from a line note to a line note, or from a space note to a space note.

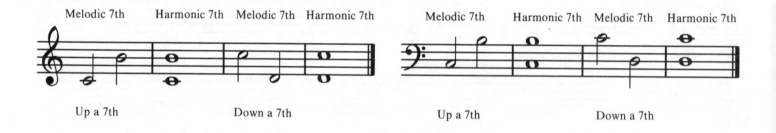

As you play these intervals, say their names.

INTERVAL PLAY

Interval of an 8th (Octave)

When you skip 6 white keys, the interval is called an 8th. It is also called an octave.

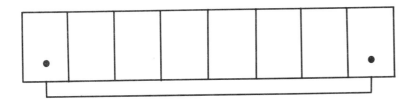

Play intervals of an octave several different places on the keyboard. Use fingers 1 and 5 of each hand. LISTEN to the sounds of the intervals as you play.

Close your eyes and LISTEN as your teacher plays MELODIC and HARMONIC 7ths and octaves. Use your EAR to identify each of the intervals.

Now LISTEN as your teacher plays MELODIC and HARMONIC 2nds, 3rds, 4ths, 5ths, 6ths, 7ths and octaves. Each interval has a unique, distinct sound that you should learn to recognize.

An interval of an octave on the staff is written from a line note to a space note, or from a space note to a line note.

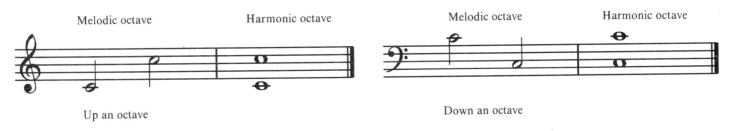

INTERVAL PLAY

As you play these octaves, say their names.

Teacher: If the span of the student's hand is large enough, this piece may be played entirely with the left hand, one octave lower than written, then with the right hand, one octave higher than written.

14

Music form is the pattern of a composition. The patterns formed by the series of notes and rhythms may be alike (similar) or different (contrasting).

BINARY FORM

A composition with two contrasting sections is written in BINARY FORM. The first section is referred to as "A." The second section is called "B." The following composition is an example of A B or Binary form.

Stems up - R.H.
Stems down - L.H.

ROBBIE, THE ROBOT

GLOVER - STEWART

SECTION A

Moderato

Rob - bie, my ro - bot, can play the pi - a - no. He

e - ven plays foot - ball and soc - cer with me.

I'd like to dance to - day, but I hear Rob - bie say,

"Some - thing must be wrong with my cir - cuit - ry."

SECTION B

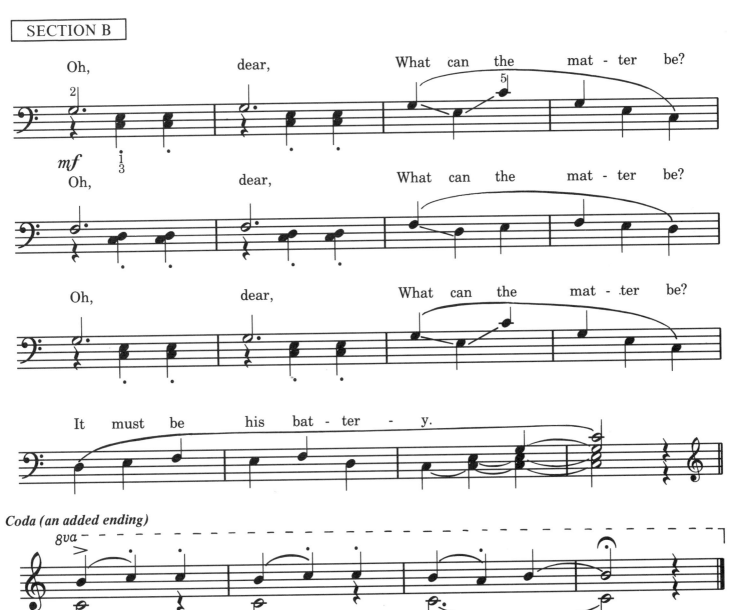

Coda (an added ending)

molto rit.
(*Molto* means much or very.)

Second Part (begins at Section B)

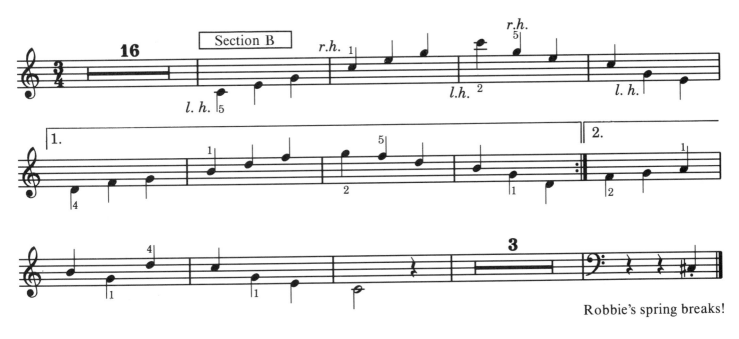

Robbie's spring breaks!

Tetrachord

A TETRACHORD has four notes that form a pattern of WHOLE and HALF STEPS in this order:

MAJOR SCALE

Two TETRACHORDS joined by a WHOLE STEP form a MAJOR SCALE.
All MAJOR SCALES consist of EIGHT TONES called SCALE DEGREES.

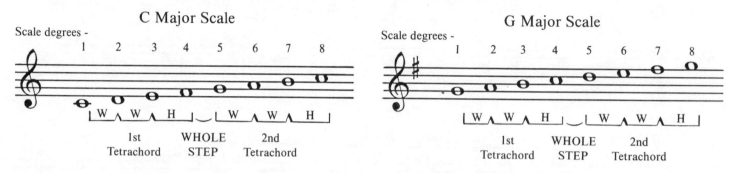

ALL MAJOR SCALES are formed by using the pattern of WHOLE STEPS and HALF STEPS as shown above.

Playing Major Scales

When playing scales, gently hold your fingers in a curved shape. Your wrist should be relaxed and level with your forearm. Always think about the sound you wish to produce before you play. Practicing scales with your eyes closed is highly recommended.

First practice slowly, gradually increasing the tempo. It is recommended that a metronome be used.

C Major

G Major

F Major

JOY TO THE WORLD

Stems up - R.H.
Stems down - L.H.

* GEORGE FRIDERIC HANDEL
(1685-1759)

Explore: Transpose this piece to the keys of F major and G major.

* George Frideric Handel was born in Germany. *The Messiah* is one of his most famous works.

Triads

Two or more intervals played together (harmonically) form a chord. A TRIAD is a three-note chord.

A TRIAD consists of a ROOT, an interval of a THIRD above the root, and an interval of a FIFTH above the root.

TRIADS are in the ROOT POSITION when the ROOT is the lowest (bottom) note. The letter name of the ROOT is also the name of the triad.

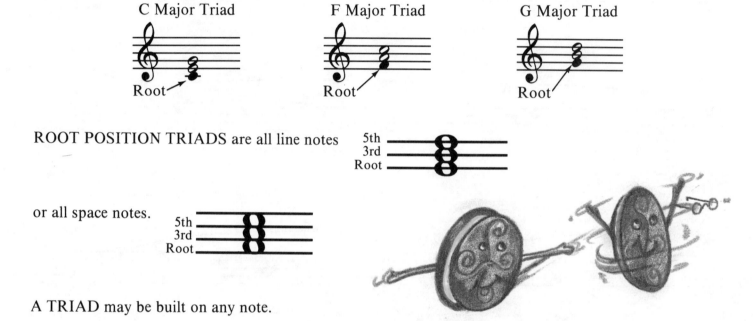

C Major Triad   F Major Triad   G Major Triad

Root   Root   Root

ROOT POSITION TRIADS are all line notes

or all space notes.

A TRIAD may be built on any note.

TRIADS OF THE C MAJOR SCALE

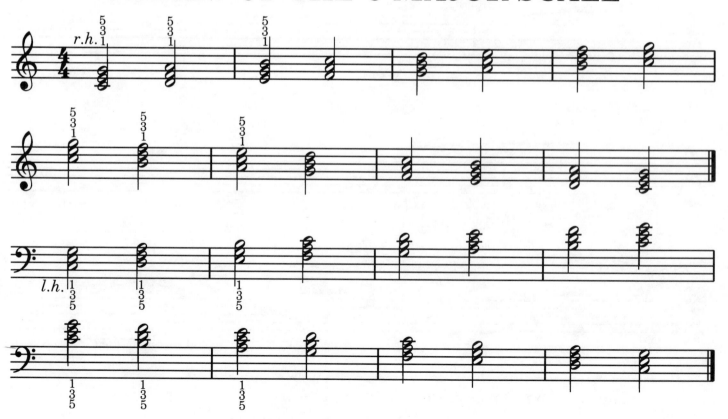

Key of _____ , Key signature _____

PARADE OF THE NUTCRACKERS

GLOVER - STEWART

EXPLORE: Make the sounds of a broken nutcracker. On the second, third and fourth lines, SHARP all the right hand melody notes. Where will you play E♯ ?

Primary Chords

Chords are built on scale tones.

Triads built on the first, fourth, and fifth notes (degrees) of the scale are called PRIMARY CHORDS.

The PRIMARY CHORDS are identified by Roman numerals and by letter names.

In the key of C Major the I (one) chord is also called the C chord because it is built on the first degree of the scale, C. The IV (four) chord is called the F chord because it is built on the fourth degree of the scale, F. The V (five) chord is called the G chord because it is built on the fifth degree of the scale, G.

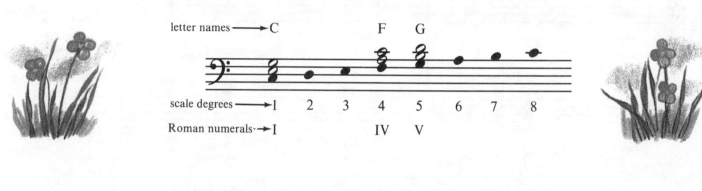

BILL GROGAN'S GOAT

FOLK SONG

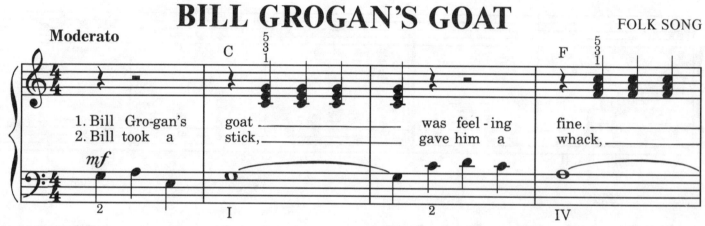

1. Bill Gro-gan's goat_____ was feel-ing fine._____
2. Bill took a stick,_____ gave him a whack,_____

1.
Ate three red shirts right off the line.

2.
And tied him to the rail-road track._____

CANAL STREET SHUFFLE

GLOVER - STEWART

Moderately slow

22

Chord Progressions

The change from one chord to another is called a CHORD PROGRESSION.

It is easiest to play the chord progression I to IV when the notes of the IV chord are placed in a position other than the root position.

The interval of a 5th above the root may be placed an octave lower to form a new position.

The IV Chord in C Major
(see page 20)

C Major Chord Progression I - IV - I

Practice this chord progression. Also play with the right hand, one octave higher.

Memorize this chord progression, then play with your eyes closed. Listen to the distinct sound of this C Major chord progression.

DANCIN'

Allegretto

GLOVER - STEWART

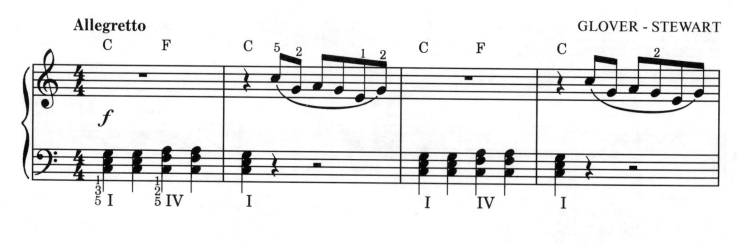

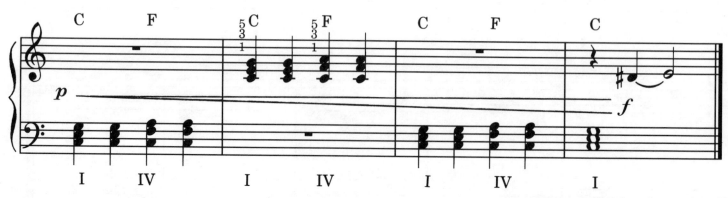

EXPLORE: Tap the rhythm of this piece as you count aloud. Do this activity with several other pieces in this book.

It is easiest to play the chord progression I to V when the notes of the V chord are placed in a position other than the root position.
The interval of a 3rd and a 5th above the root may be placed an octave lower to form a new position.

V Chord in C Major
(see page 20)

C Major Chord Progression I - V - I

Practice this chord progression. Also play with the right hand, one octave higher.
Memorize this chord progression, then play with your eyes closed. Listen to the distinct sound of this C Major chord progression.

SHORTNIN' BREAD

TRADITIONAL

Moderato

Second Part

f-p

C Major Chord Progression I - IV - I - V - I

Practice this chord progression. Also play with the right hand, one octave higher.

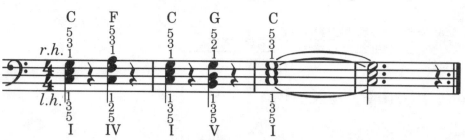

Memorize this chord progression, then play with your eyes closed.
Listen to the distinct sound of this C Major chord progression.

THE CUCKOO AND THE DUCK

Allegro

GLOVER - STEWART

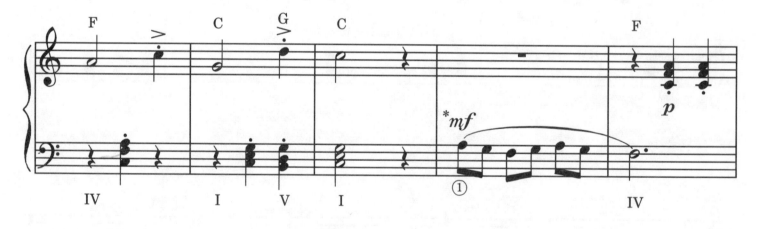

* The melody is now in the left hand and should be played medium loud. Listen to keep the right hand accompaniment soft.

EXPLORE: Change the accent from the third beat to the first beat in measures 1-8 and measures 30-38.

The V7 Chord

A V7 (five- seven) chord is often used in place of a V chord.

The Arabic numeral 7 is added to the V chord to indicate that a note the interval of a 7th has been added above the root of the chord.

F is an interval of a 7th above the root, G.

It is easiest to play the chord progression I to V7 when the notes of the V7 chord are placed in a position other than the root position.

The interval of a 5th above the root is omitted. The intervals of a 3rd and a 7th above the root may be placed an octave lower to form a new position.

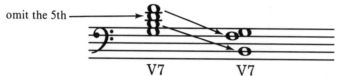

C Major Chord Progression I - V7 - I

Practice this chord progression. Also play with the right hand, one octave higher.

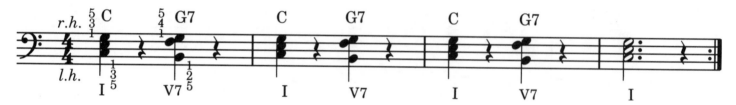

Memorize this chord progression, then play with your eyes closed. Listen to the distinct sound of this C Major chord progression.

BROTHER JOHN

FOLK SONG

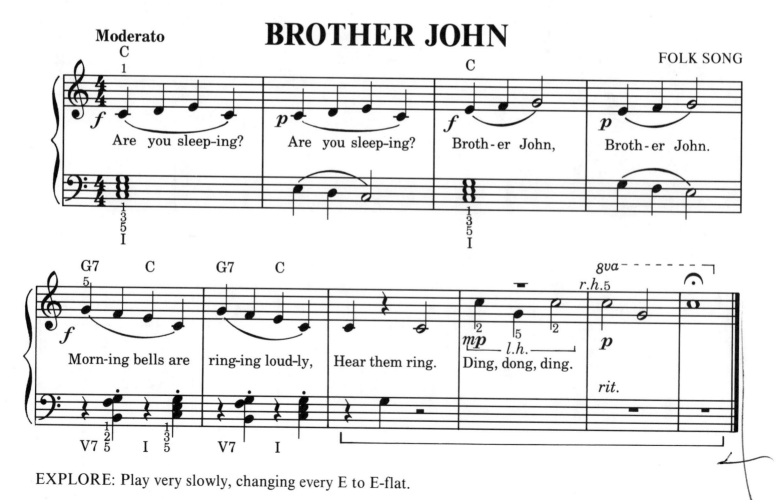

EXPLORE: Play very slowly, changing every E to E-flat.

Write the letter names of the chords above each treble staff.

* ETUDE IN C

Allegretto

GLOVER - STEWART

* Etude is a French word meaning study.

G Major Chord Progression I - V7 - I

Practice this chord progression. Also play with the right hand, one octave higher.

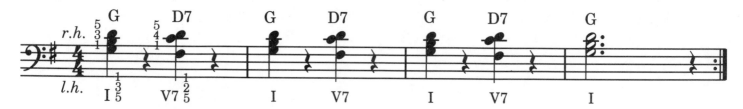

Memorize this chord progression, then play with your eyes closed. Listen to the distinct sound of the G Major chord progression.

Key of _____ , Key signature _____

SOME FOLKS

FOLK SONG

Some folks like to smile. Some folks do, Some folks do.

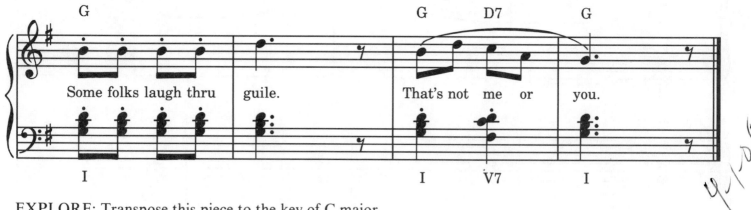

Some folks laugh thru guile. That's not me or you.

EXPLORE: Transpose this piece to the key of C major.

Second Part (Student waits for two measures of introduction then plays solo, one octave higher.)

F Major Chord Progression I - V7 - I

Practice this chord progression. Also play with the right hand, one octave higher.

Memorize this chord progression, then play with your eyes closed. Listen to the distinct sound of this F Major chord progression.

WALTZ IN F MAJOR

GLOVER - STEWART

EXPLORE: Transpose this piece to the keys of C major and G major.

Primary Chords in C Major

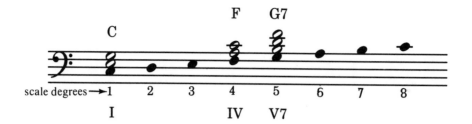

C Major Chord Progression I - IV - I - V7 - I

Practice this chord progression. Also play with the right hand, one octave higher.

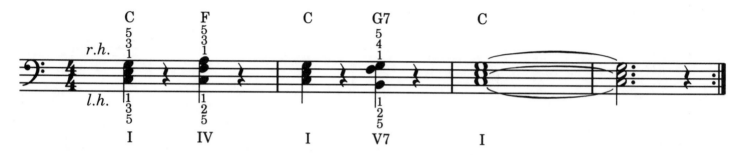

Memorize this chord progression, then play with your eyes closed. Listen to the distinct sound of this C Major chord progression.

Write the Roman numerals below the bass staff.

C MAJOR MARCH

GLOVER - STEWART

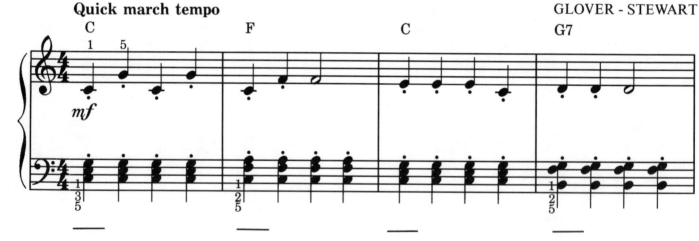

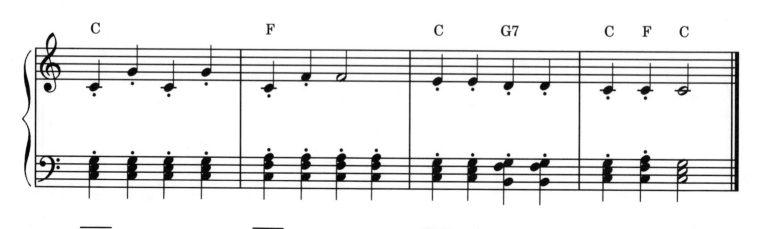

Primary Chords in G Major

scale degrees →

G Major Chord Progression I - IV - I - V7 - I

Practice this chord progression. Also play with the right hand, one octave higher.

Memorize this chord progression, then play with your eyes closed. Listen to the distinct sound of this G Major chord progression.

A LITTLE ROCK

GLOVER - STEWART

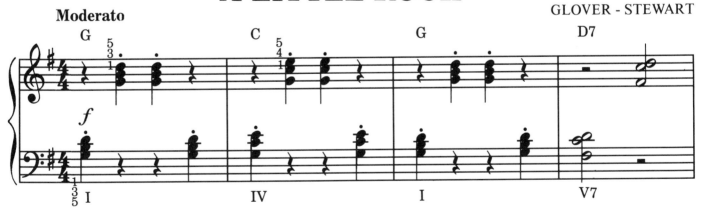

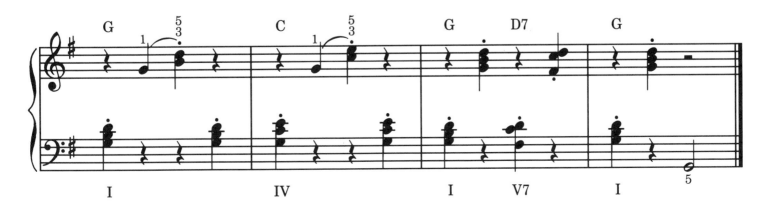

Primary Chords in F Major

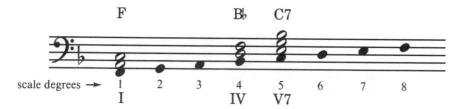

scale degrees →

F Major Chord Progression I - IV - I - V7 - I

Practice this chord progression. Also play with the right hand, one octave higher.

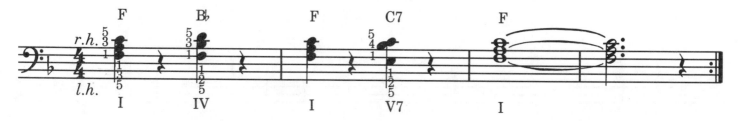

Memorize this chord progression, then play with your eyes closed. Listen to the distinct sound of this F Major chord progression.

MICHAEL, ROW THE BOAT ASHORE

Moderato

FOLK SONG

1. Mich-ael, row the boat a - shore, Hal-le - lu - jah! Mich-ael,
2. Sis - ter, help to trim the sail, Hal-le - lu - jah! Sis - ter,

row the boat a - shore, Hal - le - lu - jah!
help to trim the sail, Hal - le - lu - jah!

EXPLORE: Cross the left hand over the right hand and play the chords two octaves higher than written.

D MAJOR SCALE

The D Major Scale, as ALL major scales, is formed with two tetrachords joined by a WHOLE STEP. (See page 16 for a review of the tetrachord.)

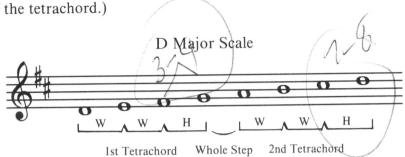

Notice that the key signature for D Major is two sharps, F♯ and C♯.

REMEMBER that ALL MAJOR SCALES are formed using the pattern of WHOLE STEPS and HALF STEPS as shown above.

Playing the D Major Scale

Remember when playing scales to gently hold your fingers in a curved shape. Your wrist should be relaxed and level with your forearm. Always think about the sound that you wish to produce. Practicing scales with your eyes closed is highly recommended.

First practice slowly, gradually increasing the tempo. Practicing with a metronome is recommended.

MAJOR SCALE REVIEW

Key of _____ , Key signature _____

A MIGHTY FORTRESS IS OUR GOD

Stems up - R.H.
Stems down - L.H.

* MARTIN LUTHER
(1483-1546)

* Martin Luther was responsible for major reformations of the church and its musical services. He is the composer of many beloved hymn tunes.

Primary Chords in D Major

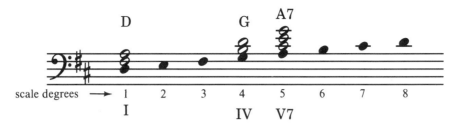

D Major Chord Progression I - IV - I - V7 - I

Practice this chord progression. Also play with the right hand, one octave higher.

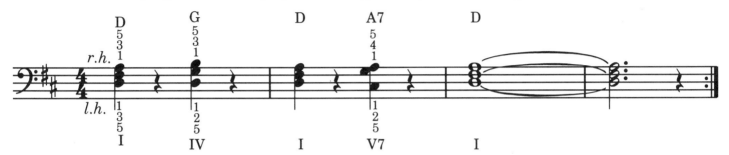

Memorize this chord progression, then play with your eyes closed. Listen to the distinct sound of this D Major chord progression.

LAVENDER'S BLUE

FOLK SONG

Moderato

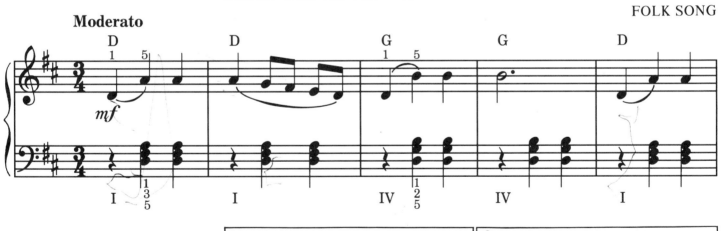

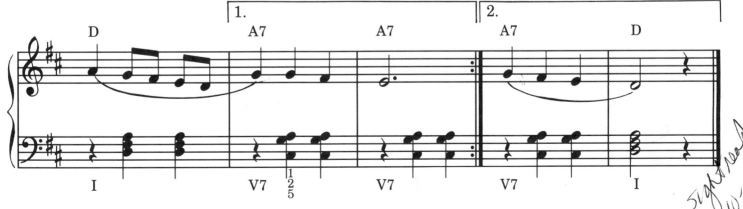

EXPLORE: Transpose this piece to other major keys.

pp (pianissimo) = very soft.
ff (fortissimo) = very loud.

Key of _____ , Key signature _____

NORWEGIAN DANCE

Animato (lively, animated)

GLOVER - STEWART

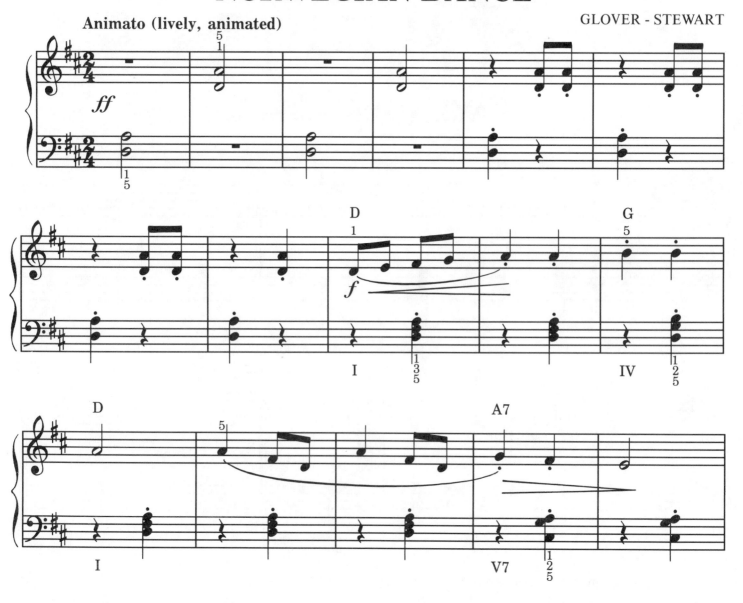

Crossing 3 Over 1

Listen carefully. Keep all tones LEGATO as you practice crossing finger 3 OVER the thumb. Always think about the sound you wish to produce before you play.

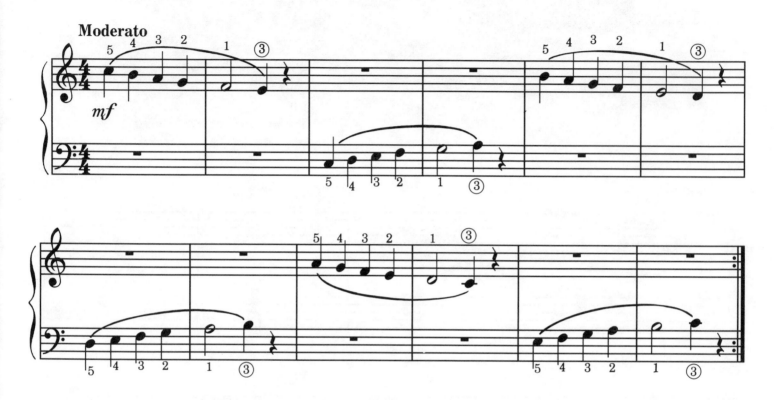

Crossing 1 Under 3

Listen carefully. Keep all tones LEGATO as you practice crossing the thumb UNDER finger 3.

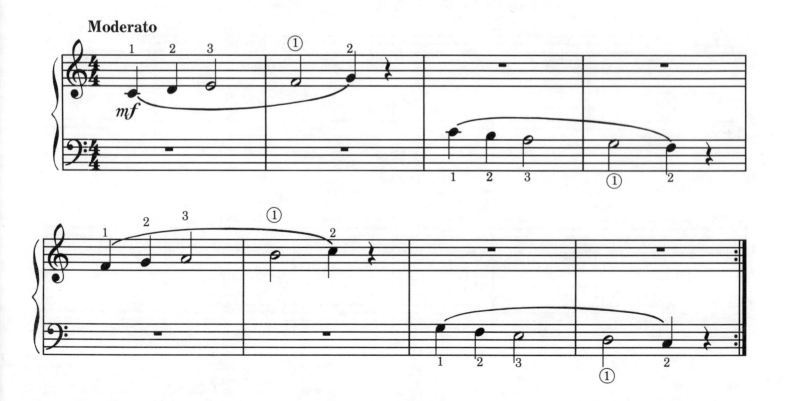

Key of _____ , Key signature _____

COUNTRY GARDENS

ENGLISH FOLK DANCE

Allegretto

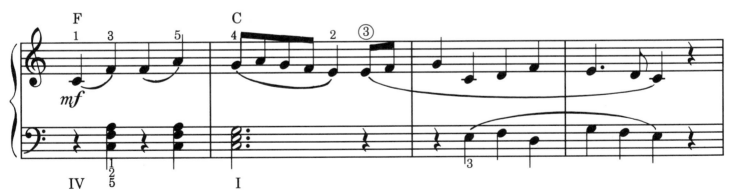

Chord Progressions

(Review)

Write key names, chord letter names and Roman numerals for the following chord progressions. An example is given.

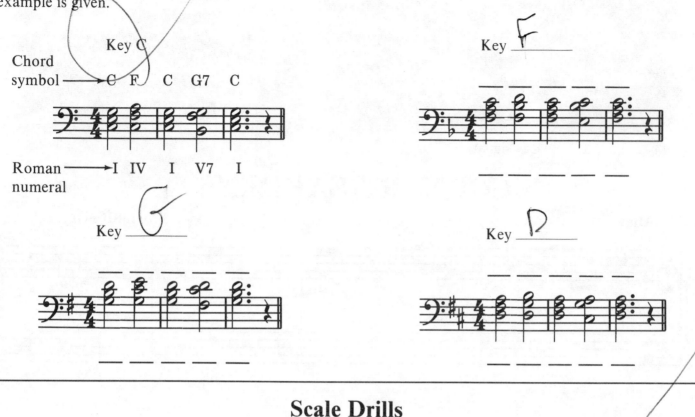

Key C

Chord symbol ⟶ C F C G7 C

Roman ⟶ I IV I V7 I
numeral

Key F

Key G

Key D

Scale Drills

Practice the following scale drills SLOWLY, HANDS SEPARATELY observing all finger numbers.

Listen carefully. Connect all tones as the thumb moves under the finger or the finger crosses over the thumb.
Remember, always think about the sound you wish to produce before you play.
Play hands together after the drills have been learned hands separately.

When the drills are secure, the tempo may be increased. Practicing with a metronome is recommended.

I.

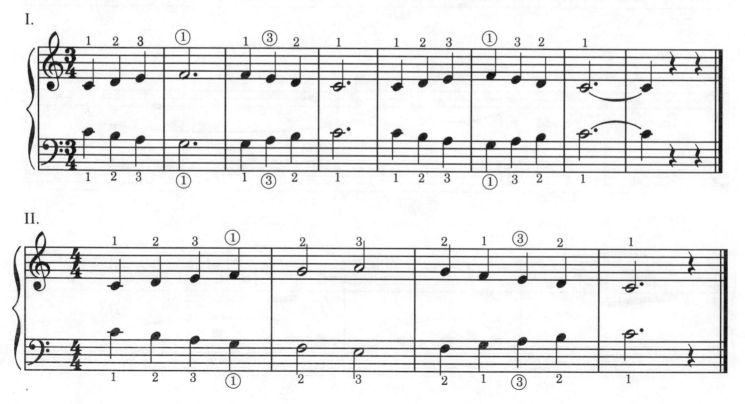

II.

TRANSPOSE the above Scale Drills into the keys of G major and D major.

C Major Scale

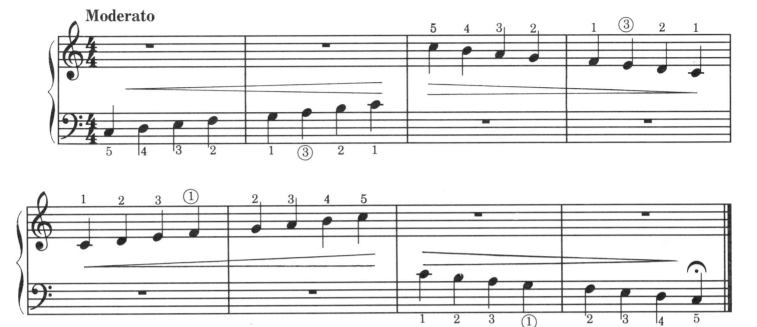

C Major Chord Progression

I - IV - I - V7 - I

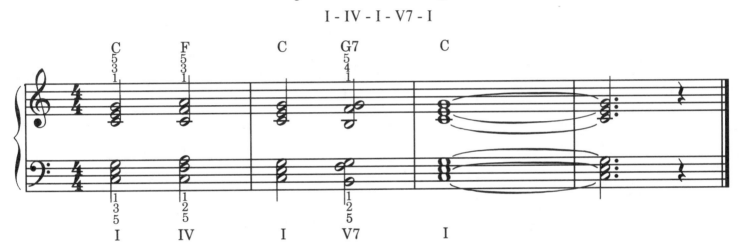

C Major Arpeggio

When notes of a chord are played one after the other instead of together, they are called an ARPEGGIO. The word Arpeggio comes from the Italian word *arpeggiare* meaning to play upon a harp.

Stems up - R.H.
Stems down - L.H.

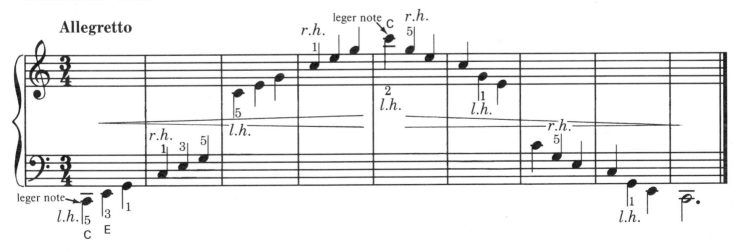

Teacher: Practice accenting different beats in the above arpeggio. The damper pedal could also be used.

Practice the scale passages of "Cathedral Chimes" <u>without</u> the pedal, carefully connecting all tones. The pedal may then be added.

Hold the damper pedal down throughout this piece.
The pedal farthest to the left is the soft pedal. Press the soft pedal down each time the dynamic sign *pp* appears.

CATHEDRAL CHIMES

GLOVER - STEWART

Hold pedal to end of piece.

(Soft pedal down)

(Soft pedal up)

The hands and pedal should SLOWLY lift as the sound of the "Chimes" drifts away.

G Major Scale

Transpose the Scale Drills on page 40 to G Major before practicing this page.

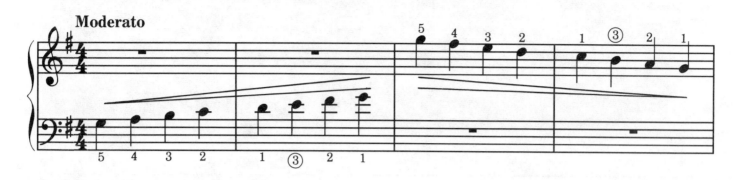

G Major Chord Progression

I - IV - I - V7 - I

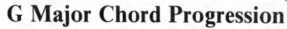

G Major Arpeggio

Stems up - R.H.
Stems down - L.H.

Teacher: Practice accenting different beats in the above arpeggio. The damper pedal could also be used.

Key of _____ , Key signature _____

SWISS VILLAGE

GLOVER - STEWART

D Major Scale

Transpose the Scale Drills on page 40 to D Major before practicing this page.

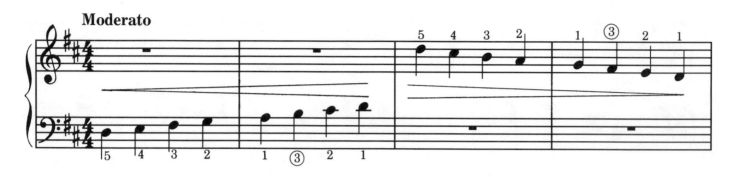

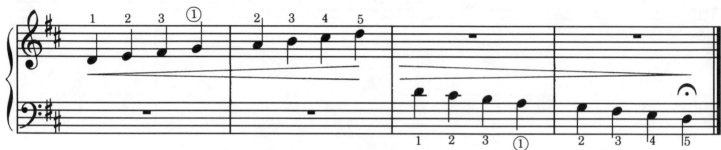

D Major Chord Progression

I - IV - I - V7 - I

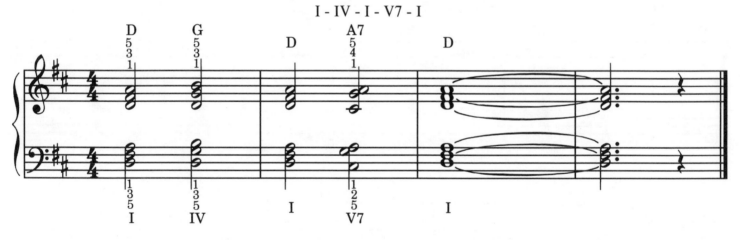

Stems up - R.H.
Stems down - L.H.

D Major Arpeggio

Teacher: Practice accenting different beats in the above arpeggio. The damper pedal could also be used.

SKATING

GLOVER - STEWART

48

Scale Drill

Follow the practice directions given under SCALE DRILLS on page 40.

F Major Scale

Moderato

F Major Chord Progression

I - IV - I - V7 - I

F Major Arpeggio

Stems up - R.H.
Stems down - L.H.

Allegretto

Teacher: Practice accenting different beats in the above arpeggio. The damper pedal could also be used.

HOE DOWN

Key of ____F____, Key signature ___i. B♭___

GLOVER - STEWART

Minor Chords and Minor Five Finger Patterns

1. When the third note of a major five finger pattern is lowered one half step, the pattern is changed to MINOR.

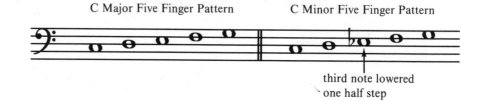

C Major Five Finger Pattern   C Minor Five Finger Pattern

third note lowered one half step

2. When the first, third and fifth notes of the minor five finger pattern are played together, they form a minor i (one) chord. Minor chords are identified by a small Roman numeral and letter names with a small m.

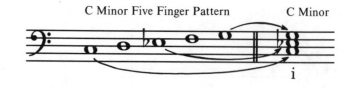

C Minor Five Finger Pattern   C Minor

i

D minor, G minor and F minor five finger patterns and chords are formed by using steps 1 and 2 given above.

D Minor Five Finger Pattern and i Chord

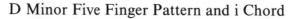

Step 1   Step 2   Dm

lowered third   i

G Minor Five Finger Pattern and i Chord

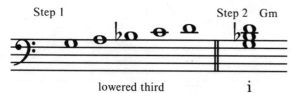

Step 1   Step 2   Gm

lowered third   i

F Minor Five Finger Pattern and i Chord

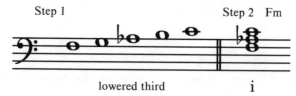

Step 1   Step 2   Fm

lowered third   i

Practice the following major and minor chords. LISTEN to the sounds of the chords as you play. Memorize these chords, then play with your eyes closed. Listen to the distinct sounds of the minor chords.

C Major and C Minor Chords

C   Cm   C

I   i   I

D Major and D Minor Chords

D   Dm   D

I   i   I

G Major and G Minor Chords

G   Gm   G

I   i   I

F Major and F Minor Chords

F   Fm   F

I   i   I

IMPORTANT: The V7 chord remains the same for MAJOR and MINOR keys.

Teacher: Minor scales and key signatures will be presented in Level 3 of the David Carr Glover METHOD for PIANO.

C Minor Position

C minor Chord Progression

THE MINOR MYNAH

FOLK SONG

When the My - nah bird sings a tune that I have heard, I can

hum a - long when the My - nah sings his song. I am

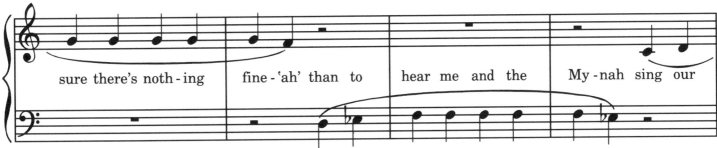

sure there's noth-ing fine-'ah' than to hear me and the My-nah sing our

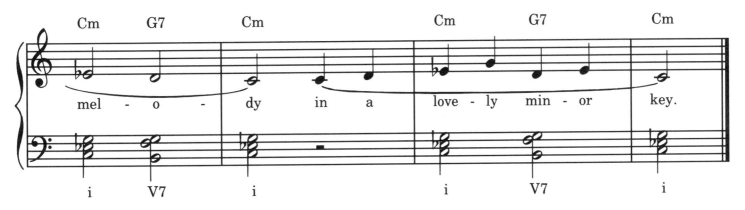

mel - o - dy in a love-ly min - or key.

EXPLORE: Transpose this piece to the key of C major.

F Minor Position

F Minor Chord Progression

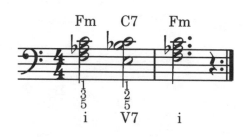

TUMBALALAIKA

TRADITIONAL

EXPLORE: Transpose this piece to the key of F major. Remember the key signature for F major.

G Minor Position

G minor Chord Progression

EL TORO!

GLOVER - STEWART

EXPLORE: Transpose this piece to the key of G major. Remember the key signature for G major.

D Minor Position

D minor Chord Progression

THE ERIE CANAL

W.S. ALLEN

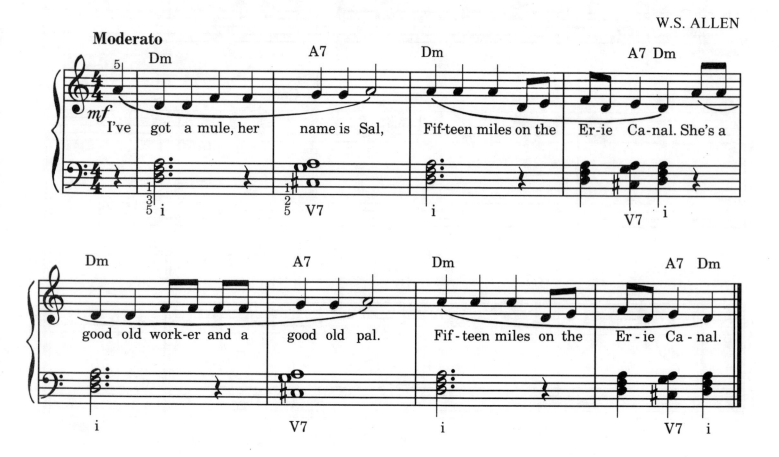

Moderato

I've got a mule, her name is Sal, Fif-teen miles on the Er-ie Ca-nal. She's a

good old work-er and a good old pal. Fif-teen miles on the Er-ie Ca-nal.

EXPLORE: Transpose this piece to C minor, F minor and G minor.

Review

1. Before each music symbol or word (Column 2), write the number of the correct definition (Column 1).

Column 1

1. Moderately loud (mezzo forte)
2. A moderate tempo
3. Very soft (pianissimo)
4. Moderately soft (mezzo piano)
5. Dotted quarter note: receives one and one-half beats
6. C major five finger pattern
7. A three-note chord
8. C minor five finger pattern
9. Rate of speed
10. Slur: indicates notes which are to be played legato
11. Added lines and spaces above and below the music staff
12. Play gradually louder
13. *Ritardando:* gradually slowing the tempo
14. Play gradually softer
15. *Da Capo al Fine:* Repeat from the beginning and play to the word *Fine* (pronounced fee-nay)
16. Fermata sign: hold the note or rest longer
17. A walking tempo
18. Moderately fast tempo
19. Octave sign: over notes play one octave (8 keys) higher; under notes, play one octave (8 keys) lower
20. Resume the original tempo
21. Slowly
22. Fast, brisk tempo
23. Soft (piano)
24. Very loud (fortissimo)
25. Loud (forte)
26. Much or very

Column 2

_____ Tempo

_____ *mf*

_____ *p*

_____ ⌒

_____ Moderato

_____ Leger lines

_____ Molto

_____ Andante

_____ Adagio

_____ *pp*

_____ *ff*

_____ Crescendo

_____ *mp*

_____ rit.

_____ *f*

_____ Diminuendo

_____ 𝄐

_____ 8va

_____ D.C. al fine

_____ Allegretto

_____ A tempo

_____ Allegro

_____ ♩.

_____ Triad

2. Name each melodic and harmonic interval. Play each interval.

Music Dictionary

MUSICAL TERM	ABBREVIATION or SIGN	DEFINITION
Accent mark	>	Play the note louder
Adagio		Slow tempo
Allegretto		Moderately fast tempo
Allegro		Fast, brisk tempo
Andante		A walking tempo
Animato		Lively, animated
A tempo		Resume the original tempo
Binary form		A composition with two contrasting sections, A and B
Coda		An added ending
Crescendo	cresc. ◁	Play gradually louder
Da Capo al fine	D.C. al fine	Repeat from the beginning and play to the word *fine* (pronounced fee-nay)
Damper pedal		The pedal on the right side that sustains tones
Diminuendo	dim. ▷	Play gradually softer
Dynamic signs		Degrees of volume from soft to loud
Etude		A study piece or exercise
Fermata sign	⌢	Hold the note or rest longer
Fine		The end (pronounced fee-nay)
Flat sign	♭	Lower a note one half-step
Forte	*f*	Loud
Fortissimo	*ff*	Very loud
Half step		From one key to the very next key
Harmonic interval		Two different tones sounded together
Incomplete measure		A measure with fewer counts than shown in the time signature
Interval		The distance between two tones
Key signature		Sharps or flats written at the beginning of each staff to indicate the key in which a piece is written
Legato		Smooth and connected tones, usually indicated by a slur
Leger lines		Added lines and spaces above and below the music staff
Melodic interval		Two different tones sounded separately

Mezzo forte	*mf*	Moderately loud
Mezzo piano	*mp*	Moderately soft
Moderato		A moderate tempo
Molto		Much or very
Natural	♮	Cancels a sharp or flat
Octave sign	*8va*	Over notes: play one octave (8 keys) higher. Under notes: play one octave (8 keys) lower
Pedal sign		Press, hold, then release the damper pedal
Phrase		A group of notes that form a musical sentence
Pianissimo	*pp*	Very soft
Piano	*p*	Soft
Pick-up		A note or notes that are played before the first full measure
Repeat sign		Indicates that a section is to be played again
Ritardando	*rit.*	Gradually slowing the tempo
Sharp sign	♯	Raise a note one-half step
Slur		Indicates notes which are to be played legato
Staccato		Disconnected, detached tones
Tempo		Rate of speed
Tie		Connects one note to another note of the same letter name to combine their rhythm values
Time signatures	$\frac{2}{4}, \frac{3}{4}, \frac{4}{4},$	The top number tells how many beats are in each measure; the bottom number tells which note receives one beat.
Upbeat		Anacrusis. One or several notes that occur before the first full measure. Sometimes also called pick-up.
Whole step		From one key to another key with one key in between

Certificate of
Accomplishment

This certifies that

_____

has completed

LESSONS,
LEVEL TWO
of the

David Carr Glover
METHOD for PIANO
and is promoted to **LEVEL THREE**

_____

(Teacher)

_____

(Date)